Divine Chronicles: Unveiling the Stories of Epic Faith Volume I

Divine Chronicles: Unveiling the Stories of Epic Faith Volume I

Developed by

Gary R. Brown

Dedication

With a sense of sadness and profound gratitude, I dedicate this book to my late Father, Willie E. Brown, and his parents, Lee Grand Brown and Elnora Brown. My grandparents played a critical role in my upbringing, instilling in me the values of faith, discipline, and love. They were instrumental in keeping me on the path of the Bible and its lessons; for that, I am eternally grateful. This book is a tribute to their memory and expresses my deepest appreciation for their profound impact on my life.

Acknowledgments

With immense thankfulness and joy, I want to acknowledge the unwavering support and encouragement of my dearest family and friends in creating my new book, Divine Chronicles: Unveiling the Stories of Epic Faith Volume I. They have been by my side from the beginning, offering invaluable insights, constructive feedback, and unwavering belief in my vision. Without their steadfast support, this book would not have been possible.

I want to credit Bible.com as the source of my inspiration for this and every Bible and faith-related project I have worked on. The Bible gives me purpose and a path to continue life and teaches me how to treat others, as it says in Luke 6:31, "Do to others as you would have them do to you."

Table of Contents

Divine Chronicles: Unveiling the Stories of Epic Faith Volume I

Preface

As I sat down to write the preface of this book, I couldn't help but contemplate the incredible significance of the Biblical figures I have included in its pages. These were not just ordinary individuals but rather extraordinary men and women who played pivotal roles in shaping the course of human history and Christianity as we know it.

Each individual has a unique story, from Judas Iscariot's infamous betrayal of Jesus to Esther's bravery in saving her people, Mary Magdalene's unwavering faith, Samson's incredible strength, and Barabbas' miraculous pardon. Through this book, I aim to unveil these epic faith figures' stories, struggles, and triumphs in a way that will inspire and enlighten readers.

By exploring the stories of these Biblical figures, we can discover valuable lessons that are just as relevant today as they were thousands of years ago. These stories offer guidance, strength, and comfort to those who seek to deepen our faith and understanding of God's plan for us.

So join me on this journey as we delve into the Divine Chronicles and uncover the stories of epic faith. Let us discover the lessons of the past and apply them to our lives today, drawing strength and inspiration from the incredible individuals who have come before us.

Introduction

The Bible is a rich source of inspiration, wisdom, and hope. Its pages are filled with stories of epic faith, courage, and perseverance that have stood the test of time. As a reader of the Bible, I have always been fascinated by the stories of its characters, from the prophets to the apostles.

I am thrilled to present my new book, Divine Chronicles: Unveiling the Stories of Epic Faith Volume I. In this volume, I explore the stories of five Biblical figures who have played a crucial role in the historic path of man and Christianity. These figures are Judas Iscariot, Esther, Mary Magdalene, Samson, and Barabbas. Judas Iscariot's story is about betrayal, which led to Jesus' arrest and crucifixion.

Esther's bravery in saving her people from genocide is a testament to the power of faith. Mary Magdalene's unwavering faith in Jesus is a story of redemption and love. Samson's strength and tragic downfall highlight the importance of humility and obedience. Barabbas' pardon is a reflection of God's mercy and grace.

Through these stories, we can discover valuable lessons that are relevant today. We can learn about the power of faith, the consequences of our actions, and the importance of perseverance. Each chapter includes Bible references to help readers connect with the stories and understand their significance. I invite you to join me on this journey as we delve into the Divine Chronicles and uncover the stories of epic faith. May these stories inspire you, comfort you, and guide you on your faith journey.

Romans 10 9–10

If you declare with your mouth, "Jesus is Lord," and believe in your heart that God raised him from the dead, you will be saved. For it is with your heart that you believe and are justified, and it is with your mouth that you profess your faith and are saved.

Chapter 1:
Judas Iscariot

Judas Iscariot is a well-known figure in the Bible who is primarily remembered for betraying Jesus. However, it's crucial to acknowledge that Jesus trusted Judas enough to grant him the ability to heal. In Matthew 10:1-4, Jesus gave authority to his disciples, including Judas, to cast out unclean spirits and heal all kinds of diseases. Moreover, Jesus chose Judas as one of the twelve Apostles, indicating that he saw something special in him.

18

Despite his eventual betrayal, Judas actively participated in the ministry of Jesus. He was responsible for carrying the group's money bag, which indicates that he was trusted with financial responsibilities. Additionally, he was present for many of Jesus' teachings and miracles. Although Judas is described as a thief who would steal from the money bag in John 12:6, this does not negate the fact that he was still learning from Jesus.

The Gospel of Judas, a lesser-known or non-canonical text, portrays Judas as a trusted confidant of Jesus, suggesting their relationship was more complex than the straightforward narrative of betrayal. This text presents a different view on Judas' role in the story of Jesus. Although not accepted by most Christian denominations, it is still worth considering. Thus, while Judas Iscariot is often remembered for his betrayal of Jesus, it is necessary to acknowledge that there were instances when Jesus trusted him. He was an active participant in the ministry.

The Betrayal

The betrayal of Jesus by Judas Iscariot is one of the most well-known stories in the Bible. According to the Gospel accounts, Judas agreed to betray Jesus to the religious authorities for 30 pieces of silver (Matthew 26:14-16, Mark 14:10-11, Luke 22:3-6). However, the story of Judas' betrayal is more complex than a simple act of greed. It involves temptations from Satan, collaboration with the priests, and the surrender of coins in exchange for the betrayal.

In the Gospel of Matthew, it is written that Satan entered Judas when he went to the priests and offered to betray Jesus (Matthew 26:14-16). This suggests that Judas was not acting of his own accord but rather was influenced by external forces. The priests, threatened by Jesus' popularity and teachings, were eager to arrest him. They agreed to pay Judas 30 pieces of silver in exchange for Jesus' location (Matthew 26:14-16).

On the night of the Last Supper, Jesus revealed that one of his disciples would betray him (Matthew 26:20-25, Mark 14:17-21, Luke 22:21-23, John 13:21-30). Judas, who had already agreed to betray Jesus, asked if it was he. Jesus confirmed his suspicion, and Judas left to meet with the priests.

Judas led the priests and a detachment of soldiers to the Garden of Gethsemane, where Jesus was praying. He identified Jesus with a kiss, and the soldiers arrested him (Matthew 26:47-50, Mark 14:43-46, Luke 22:47-48, John 18:2-11). Jesus was then taken to a series of trials before the Jewish and Roman authorities, eventually leading to his crucifixion.

Forgive Me

After the crucifixion, Judas experienced remorse for his actions and returned the 30 pieces of silver to the priests (Matthew 27:3-5). However, they refused to take the coins back, and Judas threw them into the temple before hanging himself in despair (Matthew 27:3-10).

The story of Judas' betrayal raises essential questions about the nature of free will, temptation, and forgiveness. While Judas' actions ultimately led to Jesus' death, it is necessary to remember that he was not acting alone. The collaboration with the priests and the influence of Satan suggests that he was caught up in a more extensive web of events. Nonetheless, the betrayal of Jesus by one of his closest followers remains a tragic and powerful story, reminding us of the consequences of our actions and the importance of choosing wisely.

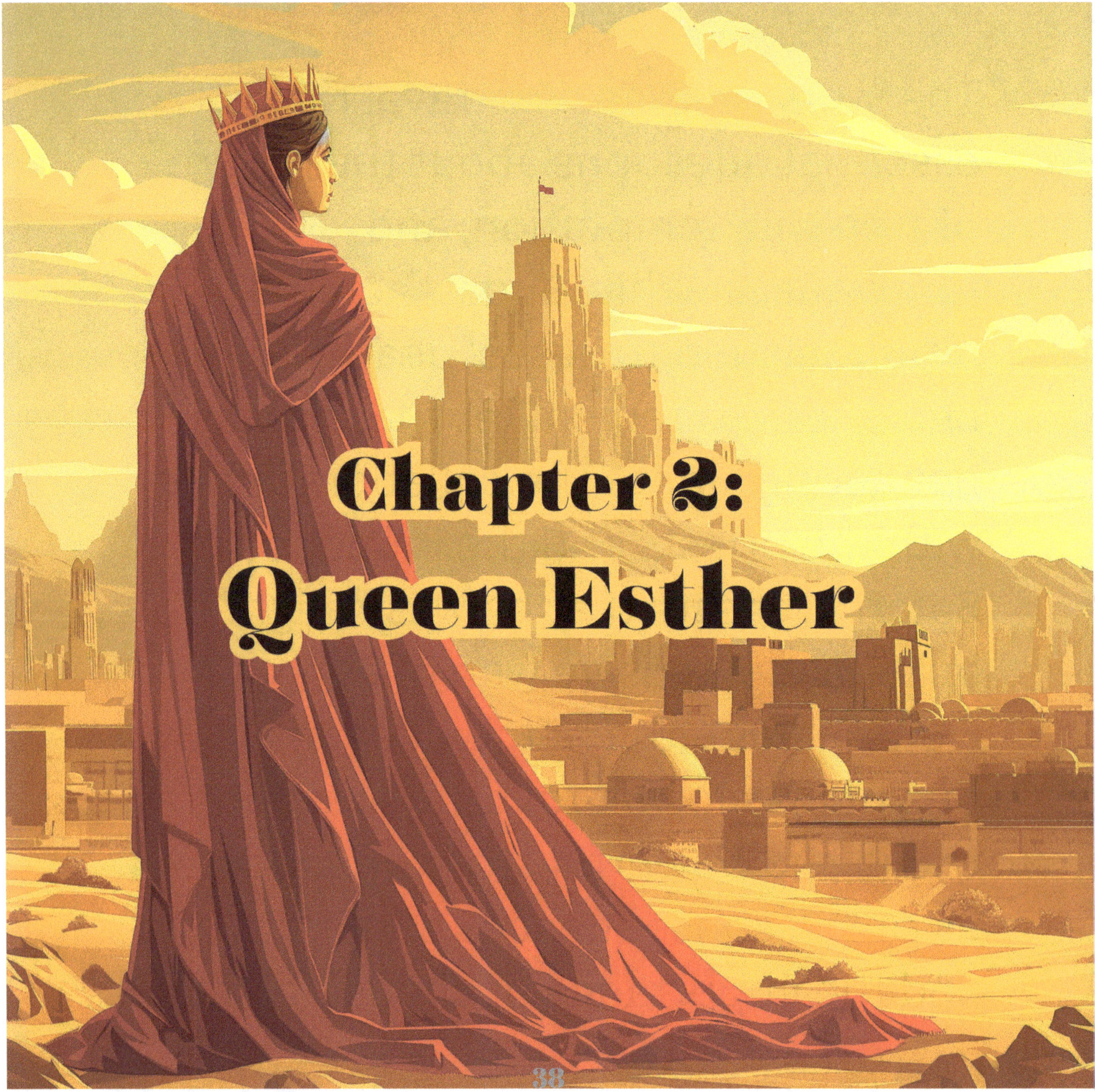

Chapter 2: Queen Esther

The story of Esther is an important and inspiring point in the Bible. It is a story of bravery, faith, and divine intervention that showcases the power of a single person's actions to change the course of history.

Esther was born in exile during the Babylonian captivity, where she was raised by her cousin Mordecai, who was more like a father to her. Esther was known for her beauty and her kind heart.

When King Ahasuerus, the ruler of the Persian Empire, held a lavish feast and commanded his queen, Vashti, to appear before him, she refused and was subsequently banished. The king then began searching for a new queen, and Esther was one of the many young women brought to the palace for consideration.

Esther's upbringing instilled a strong sense of faith and morality, guiding her actions throughout her life. She kept her Jewish identity hidden at the request of Mordecai, who feared for her safety.

When a plot to exterminate the Jewish people was uncovered, Mordecai urged Esther to reveal her true identity and speak to the king on behalf of her people. This was a dangerous move, as anyone who approached the king without being summoned risked being put to death.

Esther was torn between her loyalty to her people and her fear of approaching the king. But Mordecai reminded her of her duty and urged her to act, saying, "And who knows that you have come to your royal position for such a time as this?" (Esther 4:14).

Esther found the courage to approach the king, saying, "If I have found favor in your sight, O king, and if it please the king, let my life be given me at my petition, and my people at my request." (Esther 7:3). She then revealed the plot to exterminate the Jews. The king was outraged and ordered the plotters to be executed, saving the Jewish people from certain death.

The story of Esther is remarkable for many reasons, one of which is that it is the only book in the Bible that does not mention God explicitly. However, throughout the story, God worked behind the scenes to save His people.

For example, Esther risked her life when she revealed her true identity to the king. But the king extended his scepter to her, a sign of his favor, and spared her life. This was a clear indication of God's hand at work, protecting Esther and ensuring the salvation of His people.

The story of Esther also serves as a reminder of the importance of faith and how it can move mountains. When Esther faced an impossible situation, she turned to God for guidance and found the strength and courage to act. She fasted and prayed, saying, "Go, gather together all the Jews who are present in Susa, and fast for me. Do not eat or drink for three days, night or day. I and my attendants will fast as you do. When this is done, I will go to the king, even though it is against the law. And if I perish, I perish." (Esther 4:16).

The story of Esther has many lessons for us to learn, and it is a testament to the resilience and courage of the human spirit. It reminds us that we should always stand up for what is right, even in the face of danger, and that God is always working behind the scenes to help His people.

In conclusion, the story of Esther is a powerful and inspiring tale that showcases the power of faith, bravery, and divine intervention. It is a must-read for anyone looking for inspiration and hope in adversity.

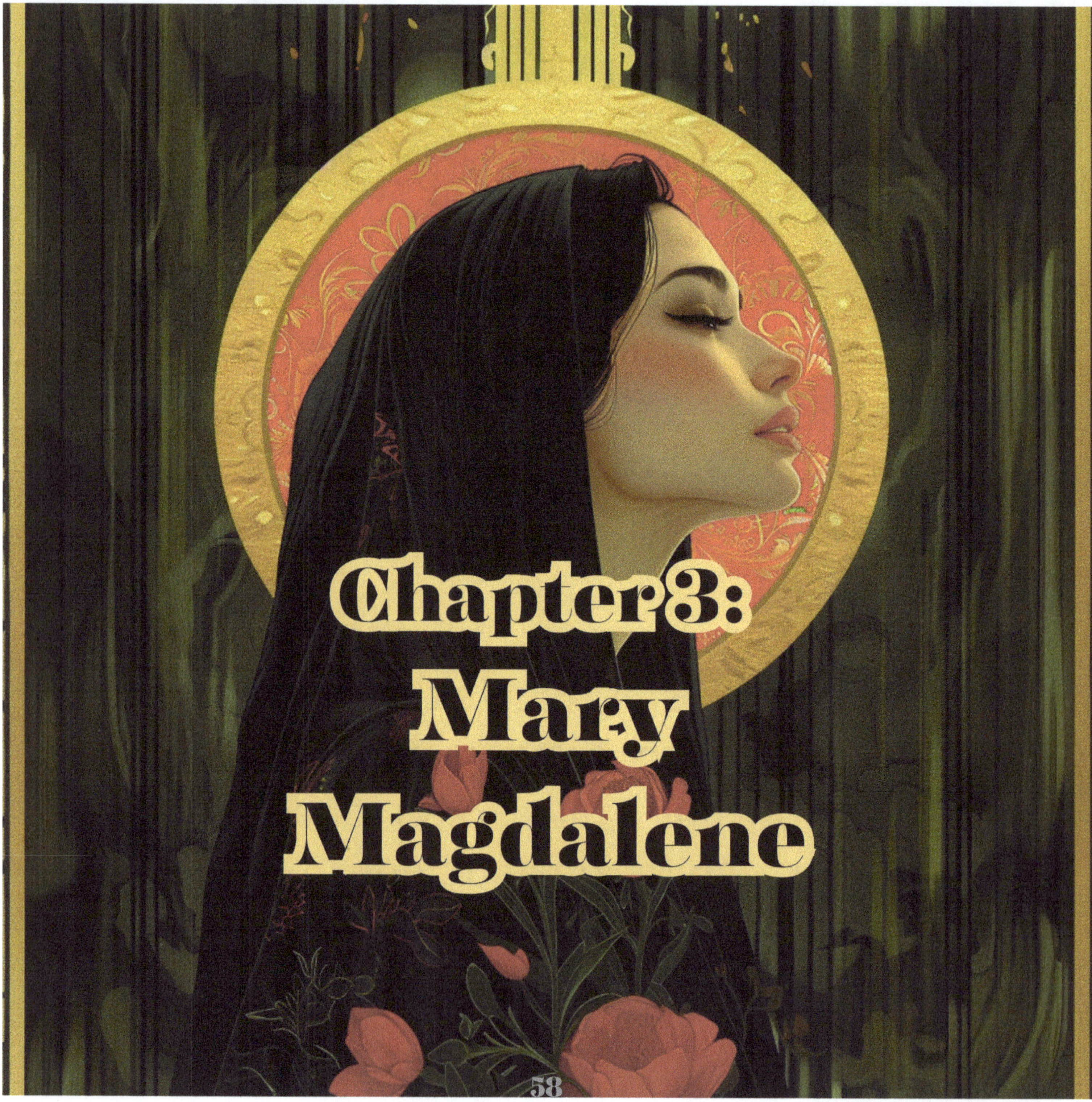

Chapter 3: Mary Magdalene

Mary Magdalene's story is a captivating account of the New Testament, and her role in the life of Jesus Christ has profoundly impacted Christianity. According to the Gospel of Luke, Mary Magdalene was a woman from whom Jesus cast out seven demons, freeing her from her afflictions (Luke 8:2). From that moment on, she became a devoted follower of Jesus, traveling with him and his disciples and providing them with support and care.

Mary Magdalene was present at many significant moments in Jesus' life, including his crucifixion and burial. She was among the group of women who witnessed his crucifixion and stayed with him until the end (Mark 15:40-41). After his death, she remained by his side, assisting in his burial preparations and grieving alongside his other followers (Mark 15:47).

Mary Magdalene is often identified as the woman who anointed Jesus' feet with perfume and wiped them with her hair, an act of profound love and devotion (John 12:1-8). This incident demonstrates Mary's unwavering commitment to Jesus and willingness to do anything for him.

Mary's story is a powerful example of the transformative power of faith. Her encounter with Jesus changed her life, and she became a devoted disciple, unwavering in her faith and love for him. Mary's life also highlights the importance of bearing witness to the truth, even in the face of persecution and adversity. She symbolizes hope and inspiration for believers worldwide, who continue to be influenced by her story and unwavering devotion to Jesus Christ.

The story of Mary Magdalene seeing Jesus in his tomb, as recorded in the Book of John, chapter 20, verses 11-18, was a significant moment that played a crucial role in inspiring the Apostles' faith. Mary's encounter with the risen Jesus was the first post-resurrection appearance of Jesus to anyone in the Bible. It was a powerful testimony that Jesus had risen from the dead, just as he had prophesied.

Mary's testimony was also remarkable because she was a woman, and in that culture, women were not considered reliable witnesses. However, Mary's testimony was taken seriously, and it became a crucial piece of evidence that convinced the Apostles that Jesus had fulfilled his promise to rise from the dead. This event is considered a cornerstone of Christian belief as it confirms the resurrection of Jesus and his victory over death.

The Angels said to her, "Woman, why are you weeping?"
Mary said “They have taken away my Lord, and I do not know where they have laid him.”

Woman, why are you weeping? Whom are you seeking?
Sir, if you have carried him away, tell me where you have laid him, and I will take him away.

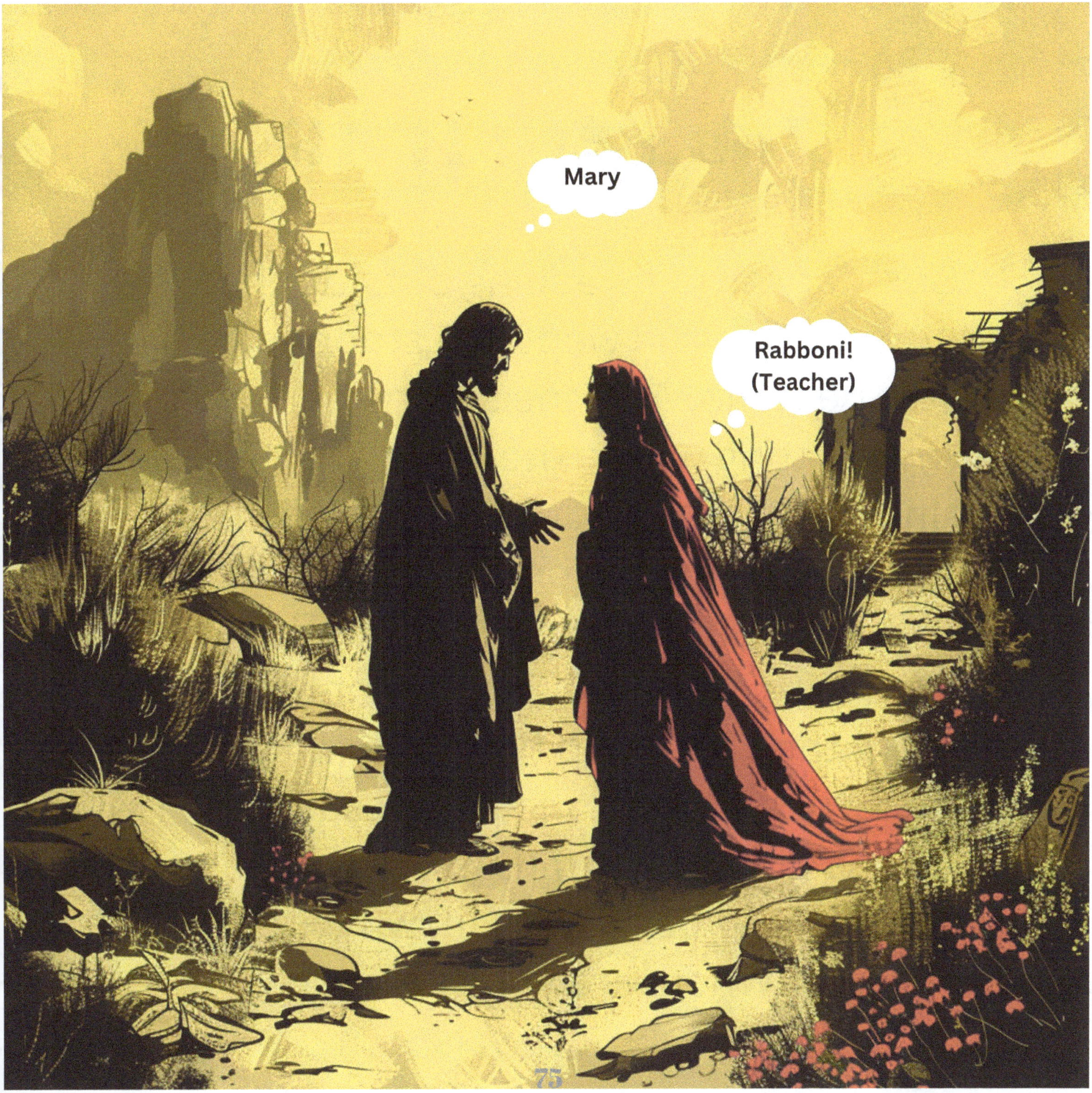
Mary
Rabboni!
(Teacher)

John 20: 11–18

"But Mary stood weeping outside the tomb, and as she wept she stooped to look into the tomb. And she saw two angels in white, sitting where the body of Jesus had lain, one at the head and one at the feet. They said to her, "Woman, why are you weeping?" She said to them, "They have taken away my Lord, and I do not know where they have laid him." Having said this, she turned around and saw Jesus standing, but she did not know that it was Jesus. Jesus said to her, "Woman, why are you weeping? Whom are you seeking?"

Supposing him to be the gardener, she said to him, "Sir, if you have carried him away, tell me where you have laid him, and I will take him away." Jesus said to her, "Mary." She turned and said to him in Aramaic, "Rabboni!" (which means Teacher). Jesus said to her, "Do not cling to me, for I have not yet ascended to the Father; but go to my brothers and say to them, 'I am ascending to my Father and your Father, to my God and your God.'" Mary Magdalene went and announced to the disciples, "I have seen the Lord"—and that he had said these things to her."

During the Middle Ages, Mary Magdalene was considered a saint and was often depicted in art and literature holding a jar of ointment or a crucifix. Many books and movies have been written about Mary Magdalene, including the novel "The Da Vinci Code." Her story inspires Christians worldwide, emphasizing the power of faith and the importance of truth. Mary Magdalene symbolizes hope and motivation, and her unwavering devotion to Jesus Christ is a compelling role model for believers today.

Chapter 4: Samson

The story of Samson is a remarkable tale of strength, weakness, and redemption. It reminds us of the power of faith, the consequences of pride, and the importance of staying true to one's calling. As we read in Judges 13:3-5:

"Behold, you shall conceive and bear a son. So then take care not to drink wine or strong drink, and eat nothing unclean, for behold, you shall conceive and bear a son. No razor shall come upon his head, for the child shall be a Nazirite to God from the womb, and he shall begin to save Israel from the hand of the Philistines."

Samson was born with a unique destiny, consecrated to God as a Nazirite. His incredible strength and mighty feats were a gift from God, but his pride and disobedience led him astray. As we read in Judges 16:17:

"He told her all his heart and said to her, "A razor has never come upon my head, for I have been a Nazirite to God from my mother's womb. If my head is shaved, then my strength will leave me, and I shall become weak and be like any other man."

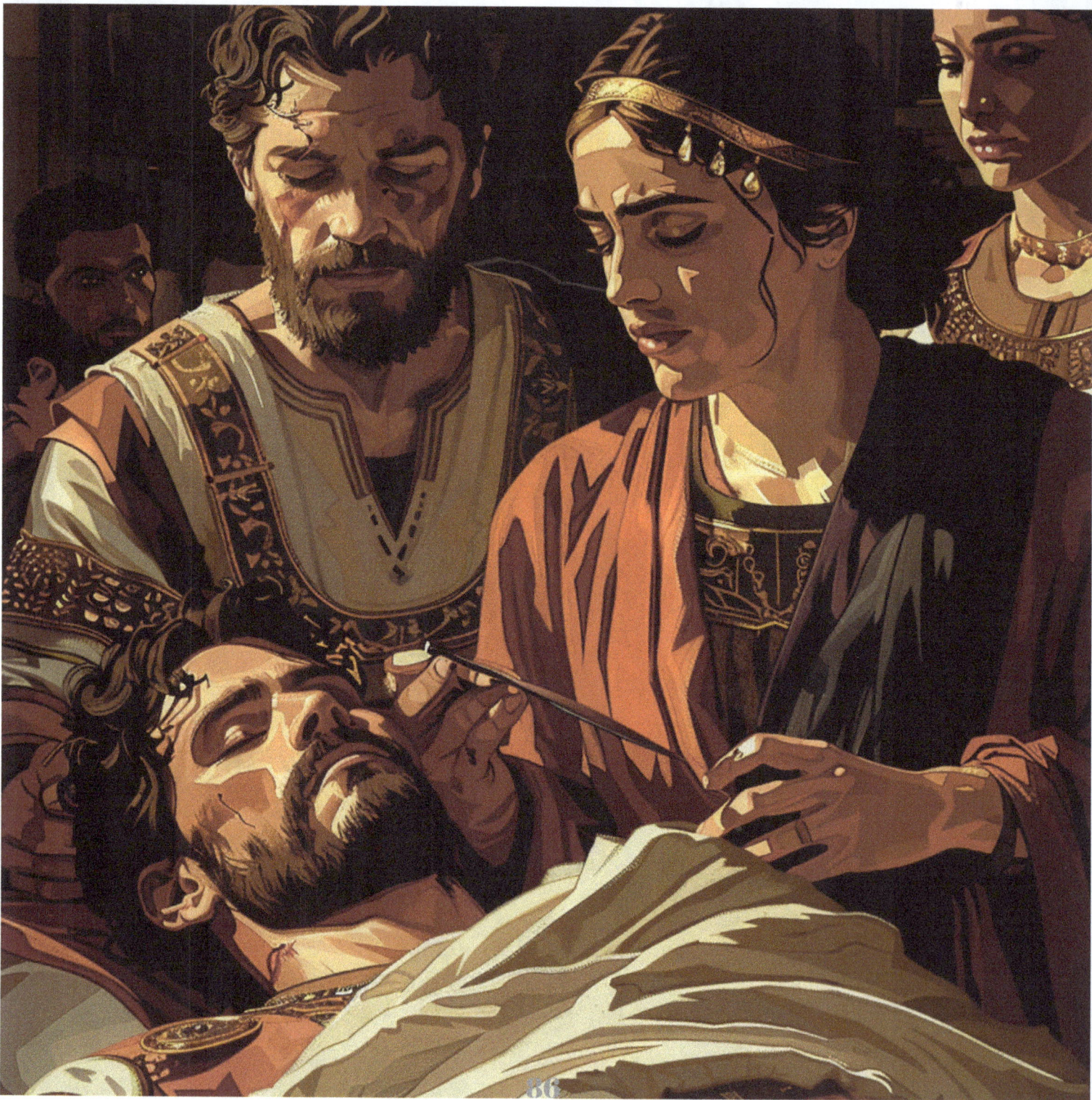

Samson's downfall begins when he falls in love with a Philistine woman named Delilah, who betrays him for money. As we read in Judges 16:18-19:

"When Delilah saw that he had told her all his heart, she sent and called the lords of the Philistines, saying, "Come up again, for he has told me all his heart." Then the lords of the Philistines came up to her and brought the money in their hands. She made him sleep on her knees. And she called a man and had him shave off the seven locks of his head. Then she began to torment him, and his strength left him."

Despite his weakness and captivity, Samson remained faithful to God and prayed for one last burst of strength. As we read in Judges 16:28-30:

"Then Samson called to the Lord and said, "O Lord God, please remember me and please strengthen me only this once, O God, that I may be avenged on the Philistines for my two eyes." And Samson grasped the two middle pillars on which the house rested, and he leaned his weight against them, his right hand on the one and his left hand on the other.

And Samson said, "Let me die with the Philistines." Then he bowed with all his strength, and the house fell upon the lords and upon all the people who were in it. So the dead whom he killed at his death were more than those whom he had killed during his life."

Samson's story teaches us about the dangers of pride, the importance of faithfulness, and the power of sacrifice. It reminds us that even the strongest and most gifted among us are still subject to human frailty and the consequences of our actions.

Chapter 5:
Barabbas

Barabbas is a name that appears in the Bible and is a character that has left a lasting impression on many readers. Born in Palestine during the Roman Empire, Barabbas lived a life filled with struggles, hardships, and crimes. He was part of a group of revolutionaries who sought to overthrow the Roman authorities and establish a Jewish sovereign state. Growing up in a tumultuous environment, Barabbas was exposed to violence and crime at a young age, which led him to become a notorious criminal.

The Gospel of Mark describes Barabbas as "a man who had been thrown into prison for an insurrection started in the city and for murder" (Mark 15:7). His actions made him a wanted man. He was arrested and imprisoned several times. However, he was always able to escape and continue his criminal activities.

One of the most significant events in Barabbas' life was his trial alongside Jesus of Nazareth. The Gospel of Matthew describes the scene in detail: "Now at the feast, the governor was accustomed to release for the crowd any one prisoner whom they wanted. And they had then a notorious prisoner called Barabbas" (Matthew 27:15-16). Pilate, the governor, asked the crowd which prisoner they wanted to be released:

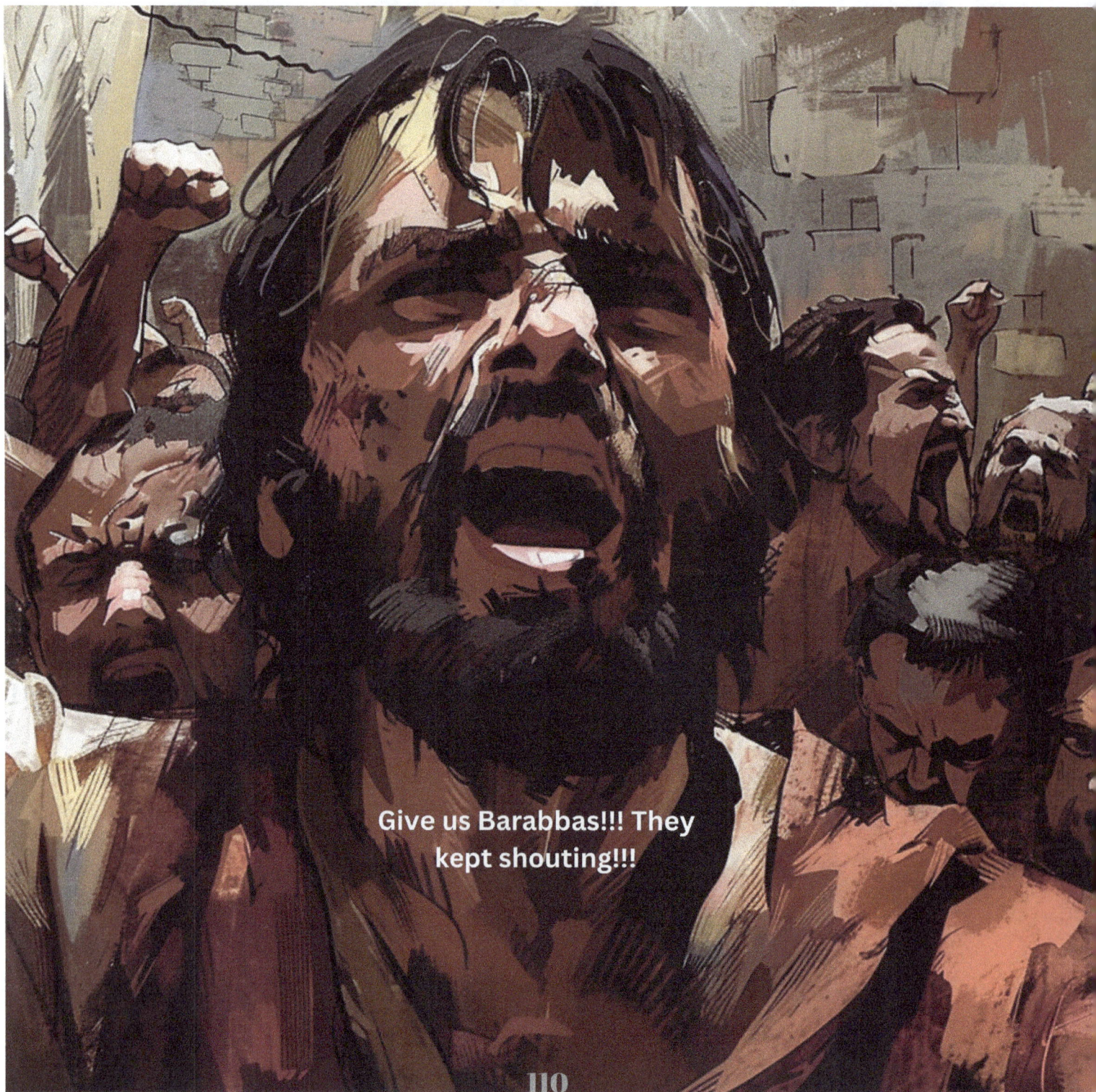

Give us Barabbas!!! They kept shouting!!!

"So when the crowd had gathered, Pilate said to them, 'Whom do you want me to release for you: Barabbas, or Jesus who is called Christ?'" (Matthew 27:17). The crowd chose Barabbas, and Pilate asked, "Which of the two do you want me to release for you?" And they said, "Barabbas" (Matthew 27:21).

They shouted back, "No, not him! Give us Barabbas!" Now Barabbas had taken part in an uprising.

Despite Jesus' innocence, the crowd chose to release Barabbas and crucify Jesus instead. This historic decision has been the subject of much debate and speculation. Some argue it resulted from political pressure from the Jewish authorities and the Elders. In contrast, others believe it reflected the crowd's desire for a violent revolutionary rather than a peaceful prophet. Regardless of the reasons behind the decision, Barabbas' life was forever changed by this event. He was set free while Jesus was sentenced to death, and the two men's paths diverged.

It is interesting to note that although it may be easy to surmise that Barabbas may have changed his life because he was not genuinely deserving of life over Jesus, it does indicate that even in Jesus' death, he absolved Barabbas for all of his sins. Was he remorseful that a simple criminal, insurrectionist was chosen over the King of the Jews? The Bible does not provide much information about the rest of Barabbas' life, but his story remains a powerful example of our choices and the consequences that follow.

An Afterword

As we come to the end of Divine Chronicles: Unveiling the Stories of Epic Faith Volume I, I hope that you have been inspired, comforted, and challenged by the stories of Judas Iscariot, Esther, Mary Magdalene, Samson, and Barabbas. These individuals are just a few of the many figures in the Bible who have left a lasting impact on the world.

One of the beauties of the Bible is that it contains a wealth of knowledge, wisdom, and inspiration relevant to every aspect of our lives. As you reflect on the stories in this book, I encourage you to continue exploring the Bible and learning more about its characters and teachings.

One of the most prominent figures in the Bible is Jesus Christ, the central figure of Christianity. He offers us salvation, hope, and eternal life through His life, teachings, death, and resurrection. His words in John 14:6, "I am the way and the truth and the life. No one comes to the Father except through me," remind us of the importance of faith in our lives.

Other prominent biblical figures include Moses, David, Solomon, Elijah, Paul, and others. Each individual has a unique story that teaches us valuable lessons about faith, courage, obedience, and perseverance.

As you continue your journey in life, I pray that you will draw closer to God and find comfort, guidance, and inspiration in His Word. May the stories in this book be a stepping stone to a deeper understanding of the Bible and its teachings.

Thank you for joining me on this journey through Divine Chronicles: Unveiling the Stories of Epic Faith Volume I. I look forward to sharing more stories with you in future volumes.

Why the Bible

I have always been drawn to the Bible for its richness, depth, and complexity. Its stories are filled with triumph, tragedy, faith, doubt, love, and loss. The Bible captures the full range of human experience and emotion, making it a timeless and endlessly fascinating text.

In my latest book, Divine Chronicles: Unveiling the Stories of Epic Faith Volume I, I delve into the stories and characters of the Bible. Each chapter explores a different Biblical figure's life and faith journey, from Judas Iscariot to Esther, Mary Magdalene to Samson, and Barabbas.

Through these stories, I can explore the themes of faith, redemption, and perseverance central to the Bible. I am constantly amazed by these stories' incredible depth and complexity and how they resonate with readers today.

One of the things I love most about the Bible is how it challenges us to think deeply about our faith and how we relate to God. The stories of the Bible are not always easy or straightforward, and they often require us to grapple with difficult questions and complex emotions. But it is through this struggle that we can grow and deepen our faith.

Overall, I find the Bible to be an endlessly fascinating and inspiring text. I am honored to have the opportunity to further explore its stories and meanings in my latest book, Divine Chronicles: Unveiling the Stories of Epic Faith Volume I.

About the Developer

PleaseLetThemKnow, L.L.C. is a small business that creates and sells books for all ages. Our product lines include Medium-content, Low-content, and original works. We primarily sell these books through Amazon's Kindle Book Publishing service. Our company was founded in March 2023. **Gary R. Brown**, a retired member of the U.S. Navy, founded a company that offers books, games, journals, and puzzle books for both children and seniors. To ensure we limit costs, we price our products based on a cost-savings structure that benefits everyone. Our main URL will always be accessible for your convenience.

If you want to learn more about my creations, please visit my website at www.pleaseletthemknow.com. Additionally, I use Midjourney to enhance the visual appeal of my book and the Grammarly app to improve the quality of my writing. Midjourney helps me enhance my images, and the Grammarly app helps me check my grammar, spelling, and punctuation. These tools enable me to focus on creative writing while ensuring that the technical aspects of my work are also taken care of. We are committed to providing high-quality products at reasonable prices. I appreciate your support!

2 Corinthians 5:7

For we live by faith, not by sight.

www.ingramcontent.com/pod-product-compliance
Lightning Source LLC
Chambersburg PA
CBHW081331090426

42737CB00017B/3092